Date: 8/18/15

J 577 NAT
Nature's places.

World Book's Learning Ladders

Nature's Places

WORLD BOOK

a Scott Fetzer company
Chicago
www.worldbook.com

WORLD
BOOK

233 N. Michigan Avenue
Chicago, IL 60601
U.S.A.

For information about other World Book publications, visit our website at
http://www.worldbook.com or call **1-800-WORLDBK (967-5325).**

For information about sales to schools and libraries, call **1-800-975-3250 (United States);**
1-800-837-5365 (Canada).

© 2014 (print, revised printing), 2013 (e-book) World Book, Inc. All rights reserved. This
book may not be reproduced in whole or in part in any form without prior written permission
from the publisher.

WORLD BOOK and the GLOBE DEVICE are registered trademarks or trademarks of World Book, Inc.

Library of Congress Cataloging-in-Publication Data

Nature's places.
    p. cm. -- (World Book's learning ladders)
  Summary: "Introduction to natural habitats using
simple text, illustrations, and photos. Features include
puzzles and games, fun facts, a resource list, and an
index"-- Provided by publisher.
  Includes index.
  ISBN 978-0-7166-7741-3
  1. Habitat (Ecology)--Juvenile literature. I.
World Book, Inc.
  QH541.14.N38 2011
  577--dc22
                                        2010022383

This edition:
ISBN: 978-0-7166-7840-3 (print)
Set 2 ISBN: 978-0-7166-7845-8 (print)

E-book editions:
ISBN 978-0-7166-4123-0 (EPUB3)
ISBN 978-0-7166-2516-2 (PDF)

Printed in China by Shenzhen Wing King Tong
Paper Products Co., Ltd.
Shenzhen, Guangdong
3rd printing May 2014

Editorial
  Editor in Chief: Paul A. Kobasa
  Associate Manager, Supplementary Publications:
    Cassie Mayer
  Writer: Shawn Brennan
  Editor: Brian Johnson
  Researcher: Cheryl Graham
  Manager, Contracts & Compliance
  (Rights & Permissions): Loranne K. Shields
Manufacturing/Pre-Press/Graphics and Design
  Director: Carma Fazio
  Manufacturing Manager: Steven K. Hueppchen
  Senior Production Manager: Janice Rossing
  Production/Technology Manager: Anne Fritzinger
  Proofreader: Emilie Schrage
  Senior Manager, Graphics and Design: Tom Evans
  Coordinator, Design Development and Production:
    Brenda B. Tropinski

  Photographs Editor: Kathy Creech

Photographic credits: Cover: © Coprid/Shutterstock; WORLD BOOK illustration by Q2A Media;
Shutterstock; p4, p19: Alamy Images; p7: AP Photo; p9, p21: Masterfile; p10, p17, p26,
p27: Shutterstock; p23: SeaPics

Illustrators: WORLD BOOK illustration by Q2A Media

What's inside?

This book tells you about many kinds of places where plants and animals live. You'll learn about the ways in which animals and plants depend on each other in order to survive in these places.

# Desert

A desert is a region that gets little rain. Most deserts are very hot during the day and cool at night. The big picture shows the Namib Desert in Africa. Animals and plants that live here have developed ways to survive in the hot, dry desert.

Sand dunes are hills made of sand. They are formed by wind.

Sometimes heavy rain falls in a desert. Colorful flowers may soon bloom after the rains.

The **quiver tree** grows only in hot places. Weaver birds build large group nests in the tree.

A **chameleon** can change color to blend in with its surroundings.

Oryxes *(AWR ihks es)* may eat melons to get the water they need.

Welwitschia *(wehl WIHCH ee uh)* **plants** can live up to 2,000 years!

This **gecko** lifts its limbs high for relief from the hot sand.

5

Forest

A forest is a large area of land covered with trees. Birds, insects, and other animals live in forests. People get wood, paper, and other products from forests. Many people also enjoy the beauty of forests. The big picture shows a forest-covered area in Canada's Yukon.

White spruce trees cover much of the Yukon.

It's a fact!
Since 1950, over half of the world's trees have disappeared.

Wolves hunt large hooved animals of the forest.

A **moose** roams the forest alone. It eats woody plants of the forest.

Elks travel in herds. They eat mostly grass.

A **falcon** keeps a lookout for food from high in a tree's branches.

Fireweed is a wildflower that springs up quickly after a forest fire.

Some scientists work to protect forests. They check to make sure forests stay healthy.

Grassland

Grasslands are large, open areas where most of the plants are grasses. Some grasslands have short grasses and dry soil. Others have tall grasses and rich soil. The big picture shows a grassland in Kenya. It is home to many living things.

It's a fact!

The Great Plains in North America is the largest grassland area north of the equator.

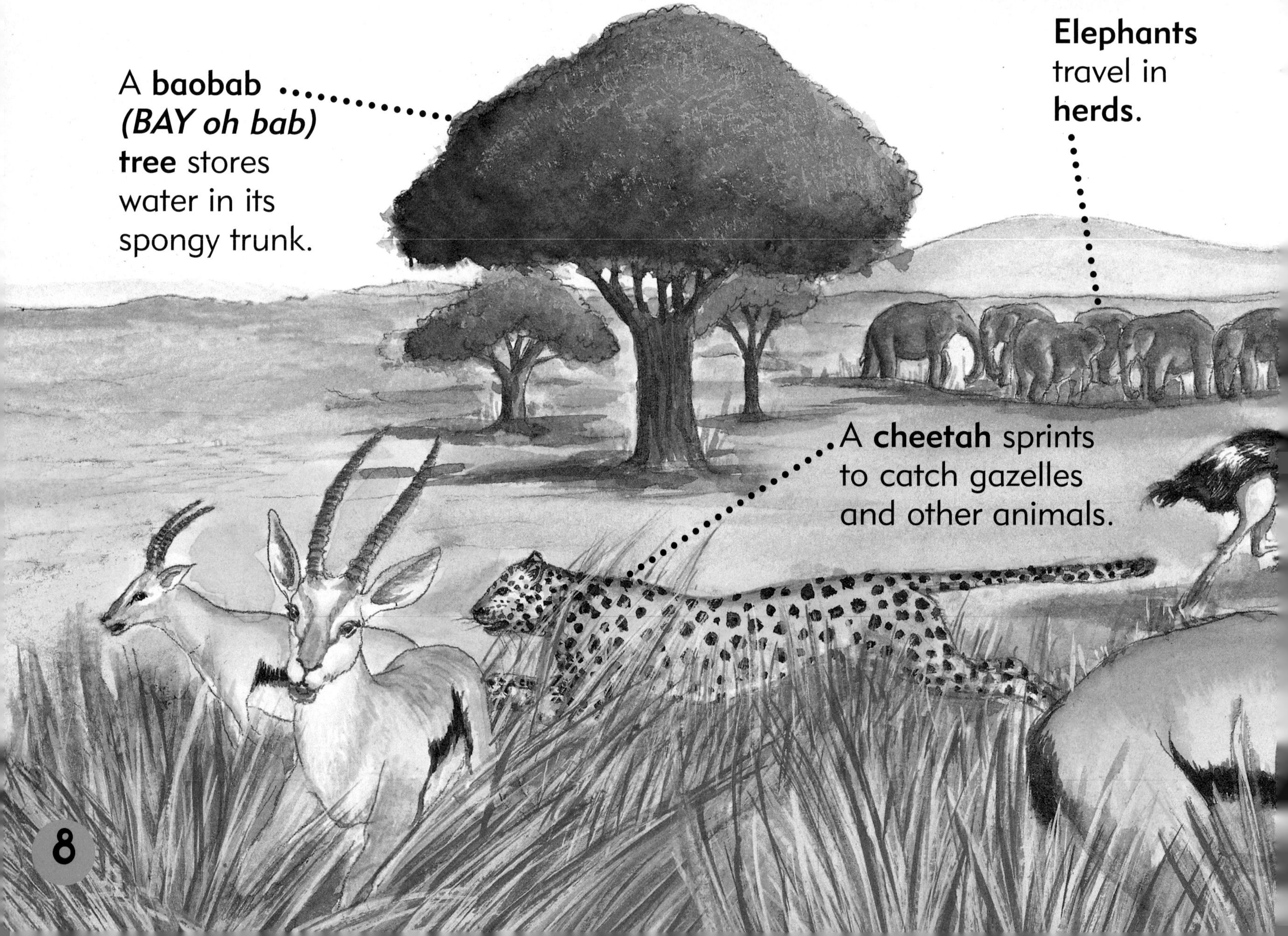

A **baobab** *(BAY oh bab)* **tree** stores water in its spongy trunk.

Elephants travel in **herds**.

A **cheetah** sprints to catch gazelles and other animals.

The Pampas is a grassland region in Argentina. Farmers raise cattle and grow crops on the Pampas.

Ostriches have long legs that help them run fast.

A **giraffe** stretches its neck to reach leaves high in the trees.

Wetland

A wetland is a place where there is usually water near or above the surface of the ground. Wetlands provide a home for many plants and animals. The big picture shows the Everglades, a large area of wetlands in the state of Florida.

Hippopotamuses spend much of their lives in wetland areas of Africa.

Insects are food for many wetland animals.

A **great blue heron** catches fish with its spearlike bill.

An **alligator** hunts small animals that live in wetlands.

The **mangrove tree** has spreading roots that help to hold the tree in place.

The **Florida panther** hunts deer and small animals in the wetlands and nearby forests.

Vacation photos

Take a look at the vacation photographs in our album. Can you tell what kinds of places were visited?

Words you know

Here are some words that you learned earlier. Say them out loud, then try to find the things in the picture.

weaver bird   **herd**   **fireweed**

alligator   **white spruce tree**

Which animals are in groups?

Rain forest

Rain forests are thick forests of tall trees. Rain forests are found in warm, wet regions. More kinds of plants and animals live in rain forests than any other place. The big picture shows some plants and animals of the Amazon rain forest in South America.

A **tree boa** hangs from a branch as it hunts small animals.

It's a fact!

Scientists believe there are millions of kinds of rain forest plants and animals that have not yet been discovered.

Rain forests are home to many different kinds of **insects** and **spiders**.

A **toucan** uses its large, colorful bill to reach fruits.

A **spider monkey** can grasp a branch with its tail.

Air plants grow on tree branches. They get the things they need to live from the tree, air, and rain.

A **poison dart frog** has colorful skin. This warns other animals to stay away!

Vines wrap around tree trunks and branches as they grow toward the sun.

Polar region

The North and South Poles are the "top" and "bottom" of Earth. Polar lands are colder than anywhere else in the world. The Arctic is the area around the North Pole. The big picture shows some animals of the Arctic in winter.

Adelie penguins live along the coast of Antarctica, the continent that covers and surrounds the South Pole. It is the coldest and iciest place in the world.

A **polar bear** and her cubs rest during most of the winter.

Musk oxen have a thick coat to ··· protect them from the cold.

An **Arctic fox** must run fast to catch a hare. ·········

It's a fact!

Most scientists believe that warming of the planet is causing the ice of the polar regions to melt.

Caribou (*KAR uh boo*) ·······
have wide hooves so they can walk easily in deep snow.

Lichens (*LY kuhnz*) ·
are plantlike living things that grow on rocks and trees. They make good food for musk oxen.

Coral reef

Coral reefs form underwater cities for many kinds of colorful animals. Coral is a rocky structure formed by millions of tiny animals. Most coral grows in warm, shallow areas of the ocean.

It's a fact!

Giant kelp is a large seaweed that forms huge underwater forests in the ocean.

A **shark** hunts the reef for tasty fish.

Giant clams are the largest of all clams.

Coral comes in many shapes, sizes, and colors.

Scientists use submarines to study the ocean and the creatures that live in it.

Sea snakes can stay underwater for hours before they need to come up for air.

A **moray eel** hunts from a burrow (hole).

Clownfish hide from attackers in a sea anemone. The anemone has stinging feelers that keep away other animals.

Tiny worlds

Many tiny worlds are right under our feet! The forest floor is home to insects, worms, and other small animals. See how many living things you can spot in the big picture!

It's a fact!

Some kinds of ants act like farmers! They grow mushrooms on decaying plant leaves.

Dead leaves provide food for small insects and other animals.

Land snails use their muscular foot to crawl about.

Many animals hunt for food in the **leaf litter.**

Tiny living things called bacteria live everywhere in the world—even inside our bodies! Bacteria can only be seen with a microscope.

Wood lice live in dark, damp places.

Many small animals eat matter from the **soil.**

Earthworms break up the soil. This helps plants to grow.

Unusual places

Some creatures live best in places where most other living things cannot survive. The animals shown in the big picture live near a hot vent along the sea floor. A hot vent is like a chimney. It sends near-boiling water into the ocean.

A fish called an **eelpout** hunts small animals around the vent.

It's a fact!

Some living things can live in extremely cold environments. Bacteria have been found deep inside the ice in polar regions!

Hot vents often form tall chimneys over many years.

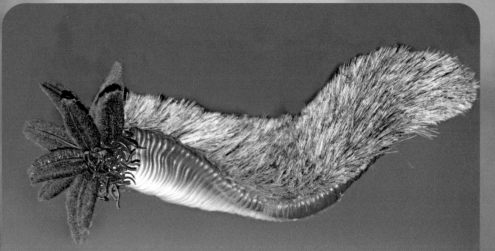

The Pompeii worm lives in hot vents in certain parts of the ocean. It can survive temperatures as hot as 176 degrees Fahrenheit (80 degrees Celsius)!

Giant tubeworms live in hard tubes near the vent. The worms poke their feathery heads out of the tubes.

Clams are food for many animals that live near the vent.

Crabs that live near hot vents will eat nearly anything—even other crabs!

Science fair

These students made projects for their school science fair. Each student is studying a special place in nature. Can you name the different places?

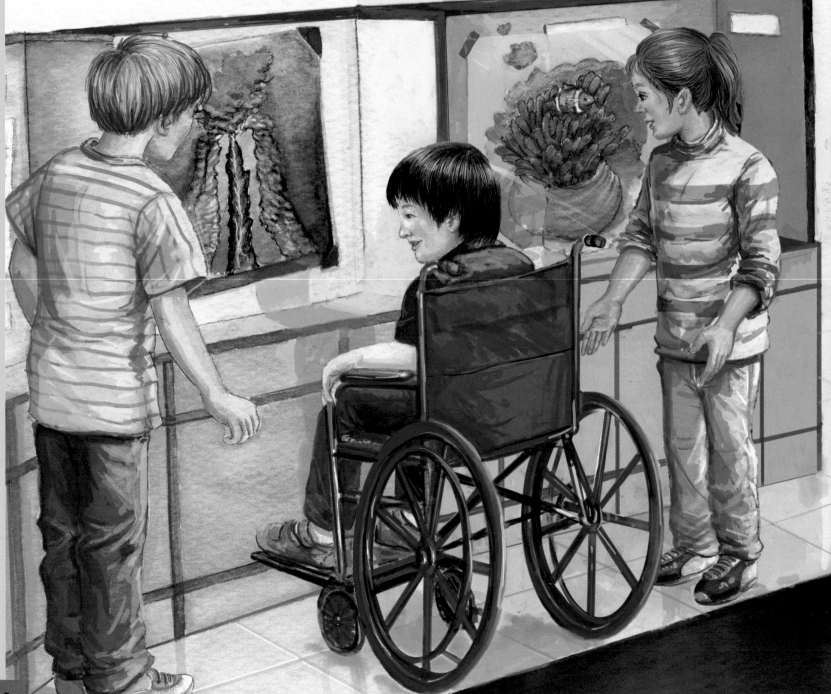

Words you know

Here are some words that you learned earlier. Say them out loud, then try to find the things in the picture.

polar bear   clownfish   hot vent

coral reef   rain forest   toucan

Did you know?

The Gobi desert in Asia is the world's coldest desert. Winter temperatures there can dip way below freezing.

The Sahara in Africa is the world's largest desert. It is about the size of the United States!

WORLD'S LARGEST DESERT

The deep sea covers two-thirds of Earth's surface. Scientists are still finding new and strange creatures that live there!

Some animals that live in the Arctic change color to help them blend in with their surroundings. The Arctic hare, Arctic fox, and ptarmigan are white in winter and brown in summer.

The southern tip of Africa is home to more than 9,000 different kinds of plants—more than any other single place in the world!

The higher up you go on a mountain, the colder it gets and the harder it is for trees to survive. Above a height called the timber line, trees cannot grow at all.

Puzzles

Close-up!

We've zoomed in on three things that are found in special places. Can you name the place where each thing is found?

1

2

3

Answers on page 32.

Where's home?

Can you match each living thing to the place where it lives? Follow the lines to find out!

alligator   tubeworm   white spruce tree

hot vent   forest   wetland

Match up!

Match each word on the left with its picture on the right.

1. frog

2. mangrove tree

3. polar bear

4. gecko

5. hot vent

6. baobab tree

a

b

c

d

e

f

Answers on page 32.

True or false

Can you figure out which of these statements are true? Turn to the page numbers given to help you find the answers.

Some kinds of ants grow their own food.
Go to page 20.

4

Scientists have identified all the plants and animals of the rain forest.
Go to page 14.

1

The Great Plains is a grassland area in North America.
Go to page 8.

5

Camels are forest animals.
Go to page 4.

2

Since 1950, over half of the world's trees have disappeared.
Go to page 6.

3

Answers on page 32.

Find out more

Books

The Coldest Places on Earth by Jennifer M. Besel (Capstone Press, 2010)
This book tells all about places where temperatures are very low. Take a journey to a hotel made of ice. Learn about a city where metal eyeglasses freeze to people's faces!

The Driest Places on Earth by Martha E. H. Rustad (Capstone Press, 2010)
Read about places on Earth where rain and snow are extremely rare.

Explore the Biomes by Kay Jackson and Linda Tagliaferro (Capstone Press, 2007). Six volumes: *Deciduous Forest, Desert, Grasslands, Ocean, Tropical Rain Forest, Tundra.* This series tells you about Earth's many different kinds of habitats.

The Hottest Places on Earth by Jennifer M. Besel (Capstone Press, 2010)
Which city set the record for the hottest temperature on Earth? What other places on Earth have extremely high temperatures? Read this book to find out!

The Wettest Places on Earth by Martha E. H. Rustad (Capstone Press, 2010)
Travel to places on Earth where rain or other precipitation is extremely high.

Websites

Mission: Biomes
http://earthobservatory.nasa.gov/Experiments/Biome/
Investigate Earth's natural communities with NASA's Earth Observatory.

Map of the Biomes
http://www.worldbiomes.com/biomes_map.htm
A colorful map of the world showing the locations of eight main habitats.

What's It Like Where You Live? Biomes of the World
http://www.mbgnet.net/
The Missouri Botanical Garden describes 12 different kinds of places in the world where plants and animals live.

World Biomes
http://kids.nceas.ucsb.edu/biomes/index.html
Find out about the weather, plants, and animals of 14 different natural regions on Earth.

Answers

Puzzles
from pages 28 and 29

Close-up!
1. desert
2. forest
3. polar region

Match up!
1. d
2. e
3. b
4. f
5. c
6. a

True or false
from page 30

1. false
2. false
3. true
4. true
5. true

Index